The Rourke Guide
to State Symbols

TREES

Jason Cooper

The Rourke Press, Inc.
Vero Beach, Florida 32964

ARTWORK AND PHOTO CREDITS:
All artwork by Jim Spence; cover photo © Lynn M.Stone

EDITORIAL SERVICES:
Penworthy Learning Systems

Library of Congress Cataloging-in-Publication Data

Cooper, Jason, 1942 -
   Trees / Jason Cooper.
     p. cm. — (The Rourke guide to state symbols)
   Includes index.
   Summary: Presents a description of and background information about the
trees that have been chosen to represent the fifty states.
   ISBN 1-57103-195-2
   1. State trees—United States—Juvenile literature. [1. State trees. 2. Trees.
3. Emblems, State.]
I. Title II. Series: Cooper, Jason, 1942 - The Rourke guide to state symbols.
QK85.CD667 1997
582.16' 0973—dc21   97–16927
                                              CIP
                                              AC

Printed in the USA

TABLE OF CONTENTS

INTRODUCTION

North America's trees are an important part of our landscapes and our lives. Trees give us beauty and shade and quiet getaways.

Trees give us timber, too, and we use it in countless ways, from decks and doors to paper and plywood. From tree sap we make maple syrup and turpentine.

Trees enrich and hold the soil, keeping dirt and debris out of lakes and rivers, and they furnish fresh air. Wildlife also depends upon trees for nesting places, perches, hideouts and food.

Of the 650 species, or kinds, of trees in America, each of the 50 states honors one kind—in some cases two—as its state tree. Some reasons for choosing a tree include its importance to the state's history or economy, its scientific value, or the number of children voting for it.

Many states adopted the same tree as other states. Oaks, maples, and cottonwoods are popular, but the most popular is the sugar maple, chosen by four states.

The state trees (just 38 in all) are a mix of cone-bearing (conifer) trees and leaf-shedding (deciduous) trees. They include the oldest (Nevada's bristlecone pine), tallest (California's coast redwood), and thickest (California's giant sequoia) trees in the world. State trees also include the dogwood, magnolia, and redbud—some of the showiest trees on Earth.

Some state trees are ornamentals, planted to add beauty to yards, parks, and streets. Others grow wild in swamps and dark forests, along prairie streams, and on deserts and mountain slopes. Hundreds of city, county, state, and national parks help protect our forests for everyone's enjoyment.

Be aware of your natural heritage: Meet your state tree and its 37 companions.

ALABAMA
LONGLEAF PINE/SOUTHERN PINE

Scientific Name: *Pinus palustris*
Year Made State Tree: 1949

The tall, stately longleaf, or southern, pine is a familiar tree in Alabama forests.

The leaves of pines are usually called "needles" because of their shape. The needles of longleaf pines, sometimes 12 inches (31 centimeters) in length, are indeed longer than those of most pines. The longleaf also has long, spiky cones, up to 10 inches (25 centimeters) from tip to tip.

Longleaf pines add beauty to the Alabama countryside, but they're important timber trees, too. Longleaf pines are harvested for paper and wood products. Their sappy resin is used for tar and turpentine. (See North Carolina, p. 32.)

ALASKA
SITKA SPRUCE

Scientific Name: *Picea sitchensis*
Year Made State Tree: 1962

Alaska's state tree is one of the most common trees in the nation's largest state. It is also one of the most massive trees in Alaska. The tallest of these long-lived evergreens stand more than 200 feet (61 meters) tall.

Like pines, spruce trees are conifers. They bear cones. Spruce trees have much shorter needles than pines.

Sitka spruces are found in a narrow, coastal band from southeast Alaska to northern California. They need mild temperatures and plenty of rain and fog.

The Sitka spruce is a valuable timber tree in Alaska. Its strong, lightweight wood has many uses, including plywood.

ARIZONA
YELLOW PALOVERDE
BLUE PALOVERDE

Scientific Name: *Cercidium microphyllum*
Cercidium floridum
Year Made State Tree: 1954

Arizona's paloverdes are shrubs of the deserts and lowlands. The yellow and blue species, named for the tint of their bark, share the honor of state tree.

Paloverdes belong to the pea family. Each species produces yellow blossoms in the spring. The blue paloverde, larger of the two, grows to 30 feet (9 meters).

Both species are common in Arizona's Sonoran Desert, where they grow along dry stream beds, called washes, and onto higher ground, up to 4,000 feet (over 1,200 meters).

ARKANSAS
SHORTLEAF PINE/YELLOW PINE

Scientific Name: *Pinus echinata*
Year Made State Tree: 1939

The tall, straight trunks of shortleaf, or yellow, pines are common sights in Arkansas.

This pine is a valuable timber tree in Arkansas and elsewhere. Its wood is hard and strong, but easily worked. It's cut from Arkansas forests for use as flooring, plywood, pulpwood, and the manufacture of turpentine.

The shortleaf pine is widespread in the Southeast. In addition to being a prized timber tree, its seed cones are eaten by birds and small mammals.

The shortleaf grows to be 115 feet (35 meters) tall. Some groves of this evergreen can be found up to 600 feet (over 180 meters) above sea level.

CALIFORNIA
COAST REDWOOD
GIANT SEQUOIA

Scientific Name: *Sequoia sempervirens*
Sequoia-dendron giganteum
Year Made State Tree: 1937

Californians had a hard choice. Rather than choose one of their ancient redwoods, they simply honored both the coast redwood (shown above) and the giant sequoia.

Coast redwoods, the world's tallest trees at 350 feet (107 meters), grow in groves along the northern coast. The mountain-loving sequoias, with trunks 30 feet (9meters) across, are found only in the Sierra Nevadas in central California. Some sequoias are 3,500 years old, while the coast redwoods are much younger—about 2,000 years old.

COLORADO
BLUE SPRUCE (COLORADO BLUE SPRUCE)

Scientific Name: *Picea pungens*
Year Made State Tree: 1939

The beautiful blue spruce is one of the giant "Christmas trees" of the Rocky Mountains. It's found at elevations up to 11,000 feet (about 3,350 meters).

Adult blue spruces are 65 to 115 feet (20 to 35 meters) tall. They often show nearly a perfect pyramid shape.

Although the blue spruce is a native of the West, it has been widely planted as an ornamental tree in the East.

CONNECTICUT
WHITE OAK

Scientific Name: *Quercus alba*
Year Made State Tree: 1947

In Connecticut, the white oak is more than a state tree; it's history! When the British king threatened in 1687 to take away a charter that promised Connecticut broad freedoms, settlers hid the charter in the hollow trunk of a white oak. The term "Charter Oak" is still well known throughout Connecticut.

History aside, the white oak is an impressive tree. It can stand up to 115 feet (35 meters) tall. It's usually broader than it is tall.

The white oak lives throughout eastern North America. (See Illinois, p. 16; and Maryland, p. 22.)

DELAWARE

AMERICAN HOLLY

Scientific Name:
Ilex opaca
Year Made State Tree:
1939

The red berries and waxy, pointed green leaves of the American holly, Delaware's state tree, have made it one of the nation's favorite trees.

The American holly grows wild in much of the Southeast, but it's best known as an ornamental. In fact, tree cultivators have developed over 300 varieties of the holly. Holly boughs are widely used for decoration during the Christmas season.

The attractive wild holly grows to be 50 feet (15 meters) tall. It has a pyramid-shaped crown. It produces a crop of berries that songbirds love.

FLORIDA

CABBAGE PALM (SABAL PALM)

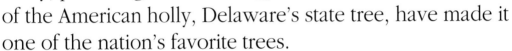

Scientific Name:
Sabal palmetto
Year Made State Tree:
1953

(Florida continued)

Floridians are used to seeing palm trees. Many kinds of palm trees are ornamentals. Florida's state tree, the cabbage, or sabal, palm is the only common wild palm in the state.

The cabbage palm is a tall, slender tree with a crown of flat, fanlike leaves. Each leaf may be as long as 8 feet (2 to 3 meters)!

The bud of the tree is called "swamp cabbage" in Florida. It's cooked and eaten, especially during the swamp cabbage festivals held throughout the state's rural areas.
(See South Carolina, p. 38.)

GEORGIA
LIVE OAK

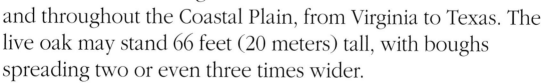

Scientific Name:
Quercus virginiana
Year Made State Tree:
1937

The grand live oak is a favorite tree in Georgia and throughout the Coastal Plain, from Virginia to Texas. The live oak may stand 66 feet (20 meters) tall, with boughs spreading two or even three times wider.

A deciduous tree, the live oak drops its small oval leaves after new ones have grown in, so the tree is "alive" all year.

Several types of air plants, such as Spanish moss, cling to the limbs of live oaks. Animals love their heavy crop of acorns.

Hawaii
Kukui/Candlenut

Scientific Name: *Aleurites moluccana*
Year Made State Tree: 1959

Hawaii's kukui, or candlenut, tree is part of the history of Hawaiian culture. The nuts of the kukui—pronounced KOO kooee—were once ground for their oil. The oil was burned in stove lamps, thus the name "candlenut." The nuts are still used to some extent for fuel and in varnishes.

The kukui's greenish-white flowers traditionally have been used in the Hawaiian necklaces called leis.

Kukui with its long, spreading branches and light green leaves, grows wild on mountain slopes. It reaches heights of 60 feet (18 meters). It's popular as an ornamental tree for its blossoms and shade.

14

IDAHO
WESTERN WHITE PINE

Scientific Name: *Pinus monticola*
Year Made State Tree: 1935

Even in Idaho, a state of towering trees and dark, dense forests, the western white pine stands out. Idaho's state tree has a tall trunk and a pyramid-shaped crown. The tree can stand 175 feet (53 meters) tall.

The western white pine is found throughout the Northwest, but it is most common in Idaho. The tree thrives on the rugged slopes, growing at elevations well above 10,000 feet (over 3,000 meters). Timber companies like this tree for its soft, lightweight wood.

The closely related eastern white pine is the state tree of Maine (p. 21) and Michigan (p. 23).

ILLINOIS
WHITE OAK

Scientific Name:
Quercus alba
Year Made State Tree:
1973

For years, Illinois regarded all of its oaks as the state tree. When it narrowed the field to one, in 1973, it chose the towering white oak.

The wood of the white oak is light colored, but there is nothing "white" about the tree's bark or leaves.

Like all oaks, the white produces acorns. Acorns are valuable food for such wild animals as raccoons, white-tailed deer, squirrels, and wild turkeys in Illinois.
(See Connecticut, p. 11; and Maryland, p. 22.)

INDIANA
TULIP TREE (YELLOW POPLAR)

Scientific Name:
Liriodendron tulipifera
Year Made State Tree:
1931

(Indiana continued)

The word "tulip" accurately describes this tree with the remarkable springtime blossoms. Each flower looks like a giant, cream-colored tulip—on a branch.

Indiana's state tree is showy enough to be widely planted as an ornamental. It's also valuable for its hard, lightweight wood.

The largest tulip trees reach 165 feet (50 meters). They grow in the Ohio River Valley and southern Appalachian Mountains.

(See Tennessee, p. 39.)

IOWA

OAK

Scientific Name:
Quercus family
Year Made State Tree:
1961

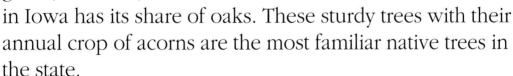

Almost every forest grove, woodlot, and fencerow in Iowa has its share of oaks. These sturdy trees with their annual crop of acorns are the most familiar native trees in the state.

Iowa has far more field space than forests, so its oaks—all kinds—are prized. And *any* oak is a state tree in Iowa. (See Connecticut, p. 11; Georgia, p. 13; Illinois, p. 16; Maryland, p. 22; and New Jersey, p. 30.)

KANSAS

EASTERN COTTONWOOD

Scientific Name: *Populus deltoides*
Year Made State Tree: 1937

Pioneers in Kansas found that trees were quite rare. Grasslands made up most of the landscape. Eastern cottonwood trees clung to the banks of the prairie rivers and streams. The broad-leaved, moisture-loving cottonwoods provided welcome shade. Early settlers transplanted many cottonwoods to their homesteads on the prairie.

The cottonwood is named for its seeds, rather than its wood. The seeds have long white threads. When the tree's seedpods open, the seeds drift away, filling the air with thousands of tiny "parachutes."
(See Nebraska, p. 27; and Wyoming, p. 47.)

KENTUCKY
KENTUCKY COFFEE TREE

Scientific Name: *Gymnocladus dioicus*
Year Made State Tree: 1976

Kentucky's state tree, the Kentucky coffee tree, doesn't produce coffee beans. Kentucky settlers, however, once used the seeds of this tree to make a drink like coffee. The Kentucky coffee tree isn't just a Kentucky tree either. It's found in much of eastern North America.

Kentucky coffee trees can be identified by their huge leaves. Some are nearly a yard (90 centimeters) long! The tree may stand 100 feet (30 meters) tall.

Its wood is used for posts, railroad ties, and general construction.

LOUISIANA
BALD CYPRESS

Scientific Name: *Taxodium distichum*
Year Made State Tree: 1963

The bald cypress, with its massive trunk and bottle shape, is one of the most impressive of all American trees. It's a well-known resident of southern swamps.

Perhaps the most striking feature of the bald cypress is its ability to send up "knees" from its roots. The knees are knobby growths that stand up around the parent tree.

The wood of bald cypress is extremely tough and resistant to water and insects. Many of the largest and oldest bald cypress forests in Louisiana and elsewhere have lost their greatest trees to loggers.

Bald cypress are conifers, but they are also deciduous. The bald cypress sheds its soft needles (leaves) each fall.

MAINE

EASTERN WHITE PINE

Scientific Name: *Pinus strobus*
Year Made State Tree: 1945

The eastern white pine is as dear to the hearts of Mainers as lobster. The eastern white pine appears on the official state seal. The tree's cone and tassel are Maine's state "flower." Not surprisingly, Maine calls itself the Pine Tree State.

In this heavily forested state, the white pine is the centerpiece of the state's huge timber industry.

In colonial days, the tall, straight trunks of the white pine were used for masts of ships.
(See Michigan, p.23.)

MARYLAND
WHITE OAK

Scientific Name:
Quercus alba
Year Made State Tree:
1941

The white oak, a strong, noble tree, is one of the most important hardwoods in eastern North America. It is found from southern Canada into northern Florida.

The broad-leafed white oak generally grows in lowlands. In the southern Appalachians, however, the white oak grows at elevations up to 5,000 feet (over 1,500 meters).

Wye Oak State Park at Wye Mills, Maryland, displays a 400-year old white oak that stands over 100 feet (30 meters) tall. (See Connecticut, p. 11; and Illinois, p. 16.)

MASSACHUSETTS
AMERICAN ELM

Scientific Name:
Ulmus americana
Year Made State Tree:
1941

(Massachusetts continued)

The American elm grows across the whole eastern half of the U.S. In Massachusetts, it has a special place in history.

Before the American Revolution (1775-1783), a mighty elm in Boston, known as the Liberty Tree, became the meeting place for colonists unhappy with England's rule. Later, British soldiers chopped it into firewood.

Now, Dutch elm disease has destroyed almost all of the mature elms in Massachusetts and elsewhere.
(See North Dakota, p. 33.)

MICHIGAN
EASTERN WHITE PINE

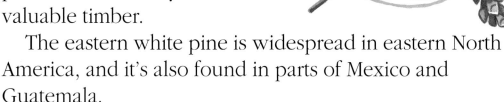

Scientific Name:
Pinus strobus
Year Made State Tree:
1955

Michigan's state tree is prized for its beauty and valuable timber.

The eastern white pine is widespread in eastern North America, and it's also found in parts of Mexico and Guatemala.

Eastern white pines are the tallest conifers in Michigan and the Northeast. The tree can reach 230 feet (70 meters), but most of the original stands of these trees were cut for logs in the 1700's and 1800's.
(See Maine, p. 21)

MINNESOTA
RED PINE (NORWAY PINE)

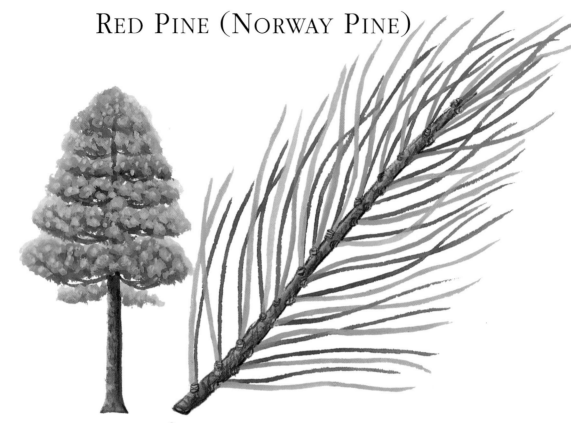

Scientific Name: *Pinus resinosa*
Year Made State Tree: 1953

The red, or Norway, pine is a native tree in Minnesota and eastward across the northern states. It may have been nicknamed Norway pine by pioneers who were reminded of pines in their homeland.

The red pine is important to Minnesota's timber industry, and it's also planted as an ornamental. Seed-eating animals, such as red squirrels, feed on its small smooth cones.

The red pine grows to 100 feet (30 meters) tall. The branches on mature trees are gathered on just the upper third of the trunk.

MISSISSIPPI
SOUTHERN MAGNOLIA

Scientific Name: *Magnolia grandiflora*
Year Made State Tree: 1938

The southern magnolia, Mississippi's state tree, is a familiar tree along the coastal plain states of the South. Few trees are more impressive than a magnolia with its showy white blossoms and long oval leaves. The magnolia, planted as an ornamental, almost looks artificial.

The flower petals on magnolias are 3 to 5 inches (8 to 12 centimeters) long. The waxy dark green leaves are 3 to 8 inches (8 to 20 centimeters) long.

Magnolia wood has limited use, but the tree is prized for its beauty. Mississippi holds the tree in such high regard that its blossoms are the state flower.

MISSOURI
FLOWERING DOGWOOD

Scientific Name:
Cornus florida
Year Made State Tree:
1955

When Missouri's spring woodlands are still leafless, the flowering dogwood blooms. Its creamy blossoms brighten woodlands and the slopes along rushing Ozark rivers. In fall, the dogwood's scarlet leaves are like candles among the muted leaves of oaks and hickories.

Dogwoods are slender, spreading trees. They produce clusters of red berries that are food for squirrels, raccoons, and several kinds of songbirds.
(See Virginia, p. 43.)

MONTANA
PONDEROSA PINE

Scientific Name:
Pinus ponderosa
Year Made State Tree:
1949

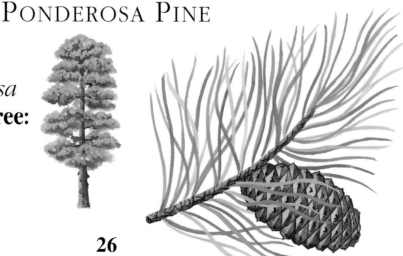

(Montana continued)

The ponderosa pine is a tall common pine of the West. In fact, the ponderosa is spread over more of western North America than any other pine.

Montanans love the ponderosa for its stately beauty. Most ponderosas are 60 to 130 feet (18 to 40 meters) tall, but the biggest of them approach 200 feet (61 meters). These big trees are up to 500 years old.

Ponderosas have an orange tint to their bark, which breaks off in "shingles." These trees are important to the timber industry in Montana and other western states.

NEBRASKA

EASTERN COTTONWOOD

Scientific Name:
Populus deltoides
Year Made State Tree:
1972

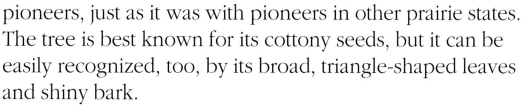

The eastern cottonwood was a favorite of Nebraska pioneers, just as it was with pioneers in other prairie states. The tree is best known for its cottony seeds, but it can be easily recognized, too, by its broad, triangle-shaped leaves and shiny bark.

The cottonwood is common along Nebraska watercourses. It became the state tree after another favorite, the American elm, was nearly wiped out by Dutch elm disease.
(See Kansas. p. 18; and Wyoming, p. 47.)

NEVADA

SINGLE-LEAF PINYON AND BRISTLECONE PINE

Scientific Name: *Pinus monophylla*
Pinus longaeva
Year Made State Tree: 1953, 1987

Nevada honors two unusual pines as its state trees. One, the bristlecone, (shown above), is probably the world's oldest living tree. Bristlecones may live to be 5,000 years old!

Bristlecones have twisted trunks and branches, as if the wind has tied them in knots. They're found in parts of Nevada, Utah, and eastern California on mountain slopes up to 11,000 feet (about 3,400 meters).

The single-leaf pinyon is a low, spreading pine. It grows in dry mountainous areas up to 7,800 feet (over 2,350 meters). Nevada pioneers used the pinyon's seeds for food and the wood for mine shafts.

NEW HAMPSHIRE
WHITE BIRCH (PAPER BIRCH)

Scientific Name: *Betula papyrifera*
Year Made State Tree: 1947

The tall, slender white birch, New Hampshire's state tree, is well known for its papery white bark. The bark peels quite easily, and Native americans once built canoes of white birch bark. Peeling bark from the tree, however, can kill it.

White birch, a deciduous tree, drops its yellow autumn leaves in October. The tree usually shares the forest with evergreens and other deciduous trees, though a few pure stands of white birch grow in New Hampshire.

White birch is found from Alaska east into northeast Canada and across several northern states. The wood is used for pulp, fuel, and wood veneer.

NEW JERSEY
NORTHERN RED OAK

Scientific Name: *Quercus rubra*
Year Made State Tree: 1950

New Jersey's state tree, the northern red oak, is a favorite for shade and lumber. This big, wide tree, which can stand 90 feet (27 meters) tall, supplies plenty of shade—and acorns. The acorn crop is welcomed by insects and many larger animals, such as squirrels, white-tailed deer, and wild turkeys.

Red oak leaves turn brownish in the fall, not red. New leaves—leaflets—each spring are reddish, as is the lumber.

New Mexico
Pinyon/Nut Pine

Scientific Name: *Pinus edulis*
Year Made State Tree: 1949

The state tree of New Mexico, the pinyon, or nut pine, is a rugged tree. This small pine rarely grows to heights more than 35 feet (11 meters), but it's a wonder that it grows at all. The pinyon loves dry, rocky land and mountain slopes to 7,800 feet (more than 2,350 meters).

The pinyon produces nutlike seeds. They were formerly important in the diet of Navajo people in the Southwest. Some people still collect the seeds and burn pinyon logs.

NEW YORK
SUGAR MAPLE

Scientific Name:
Acer saccharum
Year Made State Tree:
1956

The sugar maple is a strikingly beautiful deciduous tree of eastern North America. Four states—New York, Vermont (p. 42), West Virginia (p. 45), and Wisconsin (p.46)—have chosen it for their state tree.

The broad, rounded crown of the sugar maple casts summer shade. In autumn, the leaves turn bright yellow or red, depending upon the tree's location.

NORTH CAROLINA
LONGLEAF PINE/SOUTHERN PINE

Scientific Name:
Pinus palustris
Year Made State Tree:
1963

(North Carolina continued)

North Carolina chose the longleaf pine for its state tree because it is well-known in the state and very important. The longleaf produces strong, hard, long-lasting wood for the timber industry. Longleaf pines are true trees of the South. They grow along the coastal plain from West Virginia south to Florida and west to Texas.

These tall, fire-resistant pines can grow to heights of 130 feet (39 meters).
(See Alabama, p. 5.)

NORTH DAKOTA
AMERICAN ELM

Scientific Name:
 Ulmus americana
Year Made State Tree:
 1941

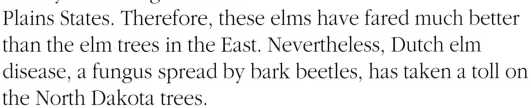

North Dakota's American elms are scattered, as they are throughout the Plains States. Therefore, these elms have fared much better than the elm trees in the East. Nevertheless, Dutch elm disease, a fungus spread by bark beetles, has taken a toll on the North Dakota trees.

Starting in 1930, the disease moved rapidly from east to west, leaving gray, lifeless skeletons where sturdy elms once stood. Recently, scientists produced two varieties of American elm that resist Dutch elm disease.

Ohio
Buckeye

Scientific Name: *Aesculus glabra*
Year Made State Tree: 1953

Buckeye trees are found in much of the east central United States. In most places they don't draw much attention. In Ohio, however, they're not only the state tree, they are also the state symbol. Ohio is the Buckeye State, and Ohio State University's athletic teams are called Buckeyes.

The tree is fairly small, commonly 30 to 50 feet (9 to 15 meters) tall. It wears clusters of greenish-yellow flowers in spring that develop into leathery seed capsules.

In some places the buckeye is known as the "stinking" buckeye. The tree's leaves, twigs, and bark have a strong odor if they're crushed.

OKLAHOMA
EASTERN REDBUD

Scientific Name: *Cercis canadensis*
Year Made State Tree: 1937

Oklahoma's state tree, the eastern redbud "announces" spring with pink blossoms. Throughout the eastern half of Oklahoma and elsewhere over its range in the central and eastern United States, the redbud brightens woodlands, parks, and yards.

Redbud is a small, short-lived tree. It rarely grows over 25 feet (7 1/2 meters) tall. It has slender, spreading branches and dark, smooth bark that contrasts with its tiny pink flowers.

Redbud is a legume, the family of plants that includes peas. The paloverdes (Arizona) and Kentucky coffee tree are also legumes.

OREGON
DOUGLAS FIR

Scientific Name:
Pseudotsuga menziesii
Year Made State Tree:
1939

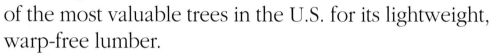

Oregon's state tree, the Douglas fir, is one of the most valuable trees in the U.S. for its lightweight, warp-free lumber.

Big Doug firs 200 feet (61 meters) tall—even 300 feet (91 meters) tall—grow in mixed forests with other Western conifers and also in mostly pure stands. Only California's redwoods and sequoias are larger.

Oregon, the leading timber state, counts forests of 1,000-year-old "Doug" firs among its natural wonders.

PENNSYLVANIA
EASTERN HEMLOCK

Scientific Name:
Tsoga canadensis
Year Made State Tree:
1931

(Pennsylvania continued)

Pennsylvania's state tree, the eastern hemlock, is a conifer, but it doesn't have sharp needles like pines and spruces. Instead, eastern hemlock has soft, flattened needles.

Hemlock is a fairly large tree, standing up to 80 feet (24 meters). Hemlock mixes with such trees as white pine, yellow birch, and spruce, but it also occurs in dense stands by itself. A hemlock can live for 1,000 years, leaving on the forest floor a thick, rust-colored carpet of decaying needles.

RHODE ISLAND
RED MAPLE

Scientific Name:
  Acer rubrum
Year Made State Tree:
  1964

Rhode Island's state tree can live almost anywhere it can send down roots. Unlike most trees, the red maple is at home in sea level swamps, in ravines, and on mountain ridges nearly a mile (over 1,600 meters) high. Rhode Islanders use the colorful red maple as an ornamental. It's a common tree, wild and planted, throughout the eastern United States.

The red maple's spring leaflets are reddish. The wide, mature leaves turn bright red in autumn.

The red maple's wood is not as hard as sugar maple, but it's valuable for furniture, flooring, and cabinets.

SOUTH CAROLINA
CABBAGE PALM/SABAL PALM

Scientific Name:
Sabal palmetto
Year Made State Tree:
1939

The tall, graceful cabbage palm is a familiar tree in the woodlands along South Carolina's ocean shores. The cabbage palm resists salty air, and it thrives in sun or shade. It can grow in forests and front yards equally well.

Cabbage palms make up the northernmost range of America's native palm trees. They are found from the Florida Keys into North Carolina. (See Florida, p. 12.)

SOUTH DAKOTA
WHITE SPRUCE/BLACK HILLS SPRUCE

Scientific Name:
Picea glauca
Year Made State Tree:
1947

(South Dakota continued)

South Dakota's state tree, a common tree in the Far North, is scarce in South Dakota. In the Dakotas, the white spruce can be found only in the Black Hills of South Dakota, where it's called "Black Hills Spruce."

Forests of this hardy evergreen once covered much of South Dakota. When the North American climate warmed up years ago, the range of cold-loving white spruce moved north. Today the tree grows from Alaska to Newfoundland and along the northern border of several states.

TENNESSEE

TULIP TREE/YELLOW POPLAR

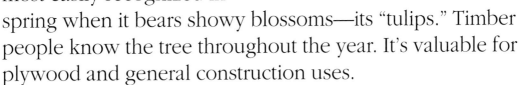

Scientific Name:

Liriodendron tulipifera

Year Made State Tree:

1947

The beautiful tulip tree, Tennessee's state tree, is most easily recognized in spring when it bears showy blossoms—its "tulips." Timber people know the tree throughout the year. It's valuable for plywood and general construction uses.

Some of Tennessee's most robust tulip trees grow at nearly 4,000 foot (over 1,200 meters) elevations.

Only two species of tulip trees exist. The second species lives in China and Vietnam. (See Indiana, p. 16.)

TEXAS
PECAN

Scientific Name: *Carya illinoensis*
Year Made State Tree: 1919

The Texas state tree is prized for its tasty nut-seeds called pecans. But pecan trees also produce valuable timber and attractive yellow foliage in fall.

The pecan grows wild in the river valleys of Oklahoma, Texas, and northern Mexico. It's also found in the Mississippi River Valley from Iowa southward.

Thousands of pecan trees are grown in orchards in Texas and elsewhere in warm climates. A mature pecan tree can yield 500 pounds (almost 110 kilograms) of nuts in a year.

A member of the hickory and walnut family, the pecan can reach heights of 180 feet (55 meters).

UTAH
BLUE SPRUCE

Scientific Name: *Picea pungens*
Year Made State Tree: 1939

Utah's blue spruce is not true blue, but some of these mountain evergreens do have a blue-green tint.

The blue spruce grows high in Utah's mountains. It grows both in small groves and as scattered, individual trees. (See Colorado, p. 10.)

VERMONT
SUGAR MAPLE

Scientific Name: *Acer saccharum*
Year Made State Tree: 1949

When the Northeast is aflame in autumn reds, much of the "flame" is in the leaves of sugar maples. Vermonters, though, love their maples for sap as well as autumn leaves, timber, and firewood.

By properly "tapping" the bark of a sugar maple, tree sap can be collected without harming the tree. Trees are tapped in late winter, when sap begins flowing freely through the tree. The sap is processed into delicious maple sugar and maple syrup.
(See New York, p. 32; West Virginia, p. 45; and Wisconsin, p. 46.)

VIRGINIA
FLOWERING DOGWOOD

Scientific Name: *Cornus florida*
Year Made State Tree: 1956

Virginians love the beautiful flowering dogwood. It is Virginia's state tree, and the tree's spring blossoms are the state flower.

Flowering dogwood grows wild in much of the eastern United States. It's also a popular ornamental tree because of its spring flowers, red berries, and scarlet autumn leaves.

Wild dogwoods grow as part of the forest undergrowth, among taller trees. Dogwood are short-lived and rarely exceed 45 feet (14 meters) in height.

WASHINGTON
WESTERN HEMLOCK

Scientific Name: *Tsuga heterophylla*
Year Made State Tree: 1947

In the moist coastal forests of Washington, the evergreens grow tall. One of those fog-loving conifers is Washington's state tree, the western hemlock.

Like other hemlocks, the western species has rough, scaly bark and flattened needles. This species, however, is the most valuable hemlock for the timber industry. It's also the tallest of hemlocks.

Pennsylvania's state tree, the eastern hemlock, is a considerably smaller species than its western relative.

WEST VIRGINIA
SUGAR MAPLE

Scientific Name: *Acer saccharum*
Year Made State Tree: 1949

Many people think of the sugar maple as a tree of the Northeast, which is famous for maple sugar. West Virginians, however, know better. The sugar maple's sap, foliage, and valuable timber have made it a popular tree in West Virginia as well as in the Northeast and upper Midwest.

Sugar maples range from Minnesota and Missouri to North Carolina, New England, and southeast Canada. (See New York, p. 32; Vermont, p. 42; and Wisconsin, p. 46.)

WISCONSIN

SUGAR MAPLE

Scientific Name: *Acer saccharum*
Year Made State Tree: 1949

Wisconsin's sugar maples grow to heights of nearly 100 feet (31 meters). Trees that large are about 150 years old.

The sugar maple graces Wisconsin yards, parks, woodlots, and forests. It often grows with other types of trees, but sugar maples dominate many of the deciduous forests of the Midwest and East.

In the Appalachian Mountains of the East, sugar maples reach elevations of one mile (about 1,600 meters). (See New York, p. 32; Vermont, p. 42; and West Virginia, p. 45.)

WYOMING
PLAINS COTTONWOOD

Scientific Name: *Populus sargentii*
Year Made State Tree: 1947

The plains cottonwood, Wyoming's state tree, is similar to the eastern cottonwood, the state tree of Kansas (p. 18) and Nebraska (p. 27). As in other Plains States, the cottonwoods along Wyoming streams were popular cooling-off places for pioneers.

The plains cottonwood is a fast-growing tree. Its growth is helped along by the moist soils in which it usually lives.

Hollowed-out cottonwood trunks were used as boats on the Missouri River in pioneer days.

The plains cottonwood rarely tops 100 feet (about 30 meters). Wyoming's tallest cottonwoods are even shorter.

Index